THE JERSEY DEVIL

WORLD
BOOK

www.worldbook.com

CERTIFICATE OF MASTERY

THIS CERTIFIES THAT

WORLD BOOK

HAS BEEN GRANTED THE HIGHEST LEVEL OF ACHIEVEMENT IN

⊷ PRESERVATION OF CRYPTIC CREATURES ⊶

Upon the recommendation of Abner Normal, president and founder of
The Society for the Preservation of Cryptic Creatures

CHAIRPERSON

SOCIETY FOR THE PRESERVATION OF CRYPTIC CREATURES

Abner Normal

PRESIDENT

Contents

How to use this book

A field guide is a book written to help you identify and learn about animals and other things in nature. The "field" part is just a fancy way of saying you're supposed to carry it with you while tramping about in the wild. A normal field guide would fit in your pocket. This one very probably will not.

A normal field guide is also filled with normal sorts of information about muskrats and mushrooms provided by normal experts. This field guide deals with the Jersey Devil, a legendary monster of the New Jersey woods. Jersey Devil experts are a mixed bag of hobbyists, hucksters, and outright hoaxers. You'll just have to deal with it.

The following items may help you in your search for the Jersey Devil:

Compass
(To avoid getting lost in the woods.)

Helmet
(The devil is a flying monster and may attack from above.)

Tick spray
(A sensible precaution in the woods.)

Holy water
(In case you run into the actual Devil.)

Caution:
If you have ever read a fairy tale, you know that it's dangerous to wander off into the woods in search of legendary monsters. So wear comfortable shoes and be sure to ask a parents' permission.

Range

The Jersey Devil is said to haunt the Pine Barrens region of southern New Jersey, also called the Pinelands. The Barrens are a heavily forested area covering about a third of the state.

Barren (infertile) might seem like a weird description for a place so dense with plant life. But European settlers called it that because the sandy soils weren't good for growing crops. So the Pine Barrens remained a wilderness, while cities, towns, and farms sprang up all around.

Description

When it comes to the wilderness, people's imaginations tend to run wild. And, it wasn't long before reports began spreading of a monster in the woods.

People began to report sightings of a devillike creature flying or stalking among the pines. The creature eventually became known as the Jersey Devil.

HORNS (OR ANTLERS)

WINGS

Anatomy

The Jersey Devil is often described as a horselike creature with hooves, claws, antlers or horns, batlike wings, and a forked tail. So it's kind of a cross between the Devil and Pegasus—if Pegasus had itty-bitty wings.

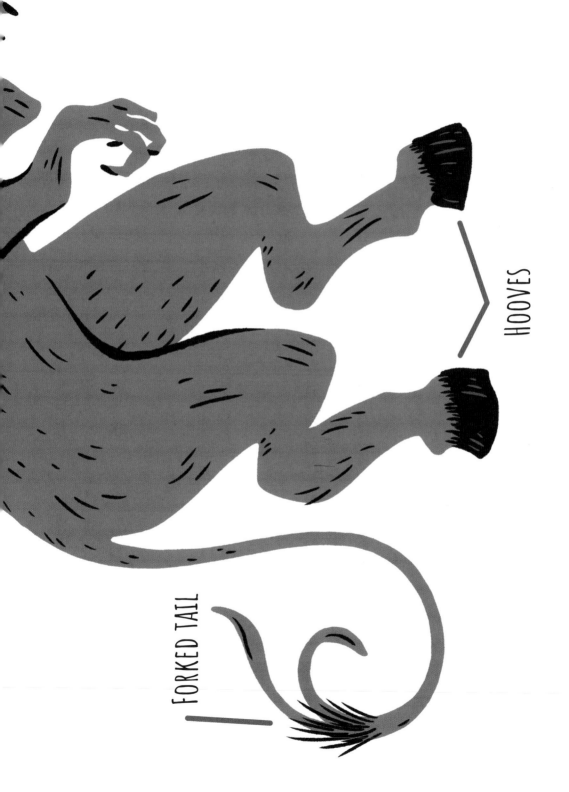

HOOVES

FORKED TAIL

People who have reported seeing the Jersey Devil never forget its sound. Some say that's because of its bloodcurdling screech. Others say it may be the creature's distinctive Jersey accent.

Everyone speaks with some kind of accent, and people from New Jersey are no exception. For example, people who have lived in the area for a long time may pronounce their a's a little differently, saying "talk" like *tawk* or "water" like *wooder*.

Origins

The Jersey Devil was at first called the Leeds Devil, and there are two stories about its origins. Here is the first:

The Leeds Devil was the 13th child of the American colonist Mother Leeds. She already had 12 kids, and she did not want another. So she wished that the Devil would take the child away as soon as it was born. The Devil held up his end of the bargain, and as soon as the baby was born, it changed into the most grotesque creature imaginable and flew away into the Pinelands.

Origins

(continued)

Here is the second origin story:

The American colonist Daniel Leeds—husband of Mother Leeds—published the first *almanac* in New Jersey. An almanac is a book of dates, calendars, and weather predictions. But Leeds apparently found this rather boring. He filled his almanac with more outlandish ideas about angels and magic. The local Quaker community did not welcome these ideas. The community was suspicious of Leeds and began associating him with devilish forces.

What's Benjamin Franklin doing here? Franklin once said, "Love your Enemies, for they tell you your Faults." But he didn't necessarily live by this motto.

Franklin was the rival publisher of the Leeds family, and he did not love his enemy publisher. Franklin and Daniel Leeds's son Titan were bitter rivals, who each tried to outdo the other with insults and rumors. In his *Poor Richard's Almanac*, Benjamin Franklin jokingly said that Titan had died and become a ghost.

Benjamin Franklin

(continued)

Titan-related lies soon became an important part of *Poor Richard's Almanac*. Franklin used his almanac to present the Leeds family as evil Devil worshipers.

The Leeds's family crest had a dragon on it. And that dragon combined with the rumors may have given birth to the legend of the Jersey Devil.

Witchcraft

Accusations of Devil worship or witchcraft were no laughing matter in the American colonies. In 1692, in Salem, Massachusetts, a minister's daughter and her cousin started having strange fits. Their behavior was blamed on witchcraft. The event sparked a panic that resulted in widespread accusations of Devil worship and other sordid activities—the Salem witchcraft trials.

By the time the trials ended, 150 to 200 people had been arrested, 19 people had been executed, and 1 man had been tortured to death. Luckily, the Franklin-Leeds feud never got so out of hand.

Habitat

Before setting off in search of the Jersey Devil, it may be helpful to familiarize yourself with various aspects of the creature's habitat.

GARDEN STATE.

New Jersey is known as the Garden State, probably for its rich agricultural production. But considering it is home to a ferocious keeper of the forest, perhaps it should be called the "Guarding State." Just an idea.

Jersey Shore.

The Shore is a famous beach and resort area on New Jersey's Atlantic Coast. But you won't find the Jersey Devil bathing on the Shore. Maybe it hates to get sand in its hooves.

Habitat

(continued)

The Blue Hole

is a pool in the Pinelands known for its striking blue waters. The hole is a storied swimming spot—the Jersey Devil has even been said to bathe there.

CARNIVOROUS PLANTS.

The Devil isn't the only monster of the Pine Barrens. The woods are also home to a variety of carnivorous plants. Bladderworts, pitcher plants, and sundews trap insects and other small mammals, digesting their bodies for nutrients.

Tracks

In 1909, a small-town newspaper in southern New Jersey reported the discovery of strange, hooflike tracks in the snow. A panic followed. People reported attacks on livestock and encounters with a monstrous creature. Armed search parties went into the forest in search of the mysterious creature. Parents were so scared that they even kept children home from school. Well, that part might not sound so bad.

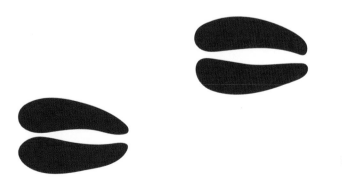

Soon after the 1909 tracks, a museum in Philadelphia claimed to have captured the vicious monster. Museum-goers eagerly awaited the opportunity to marvel at the beast. What they marveled at, however, was a live kangaroo painted with green stripes. Oh, and it had fake wings. Before this kangaroo hopped onto the scene, the mysterious creature had been known as the Leeds Devil. After the exhibition, the creature became known as the Jersey Devil.

Modern sighting

In 2015, a man reported that he had seen the Jersey Devil—and had even photographed the mysterious beast! But experts thought the photo looked more like a stuffed goat with fake wings that had been tossed into the air.

Commonly mistaken for the Jersey Devil

PINE ROBBERS

were a loose collection of thugs and marauders who skulked among the forests of the Pinelands, remaining loyal to the British during the American Revolution (1775-1783). Tales of the Leeds Devil may have served to warn colonists to steer clear of such unsavory fellows.

WHITE-TAILED DEER.

Hooves, you say? Antlers, you say? The Pine Barrens, like many other North American woodlands, are home to huge numbers of white-tailed deer.

Commonly mistaken for the Jersey Devil

(continued)

A LLAMA?

The man who captured the 2015 photograph initially thought he had stumbled upon a llama. But these woolly members of the camel family are much more likely to be found in South America.

THE DEVILS.

Think you've found the Jersey Devil? Is he holding a hockey stick? That's probably just a member of the New Jersey Devils, a National Hockey League (NHL) team that plays its home games in Newark.

Jersey Devil dos and don'ts

DO ROCK OUT WITH THE JERSEY DEVIL.

New Jersey is home to a number of the most popular rock and roll acts ever. It's possible the Devil's heart swells with pride for his fellow New Jerseyites Bon Jovi and Bruce Springsteen. The Jersey Devil was, after all, "Born to Run."

(continued)

DON'T ASSUME THE JERSEY DEVIL IS INVOLVED IN ORGANIZED CRIME.

Many people associate New Jersey with the Mafia, an organized crime syndicate with roots in Sicily. But that's just a stereotype, so fuhgeddabout it!

Classification

With no physical evidence for the Jersey Devil, it's hard to say exactly what the creature may be. Stories of its origins point to some kind of demon or spirit. But tales of encounters with the Jersey Devil make it sound more like a physical creature.

Maybe the Jersey Devil's closest relative is the bogeyman. A bogeyman is an evil creature invented by adults to scare children into good behavior. The message, in this case: **STAY OUT OF THE WOODS!**

Status

Extinct! Or rather, never existed. Tales of the
Leeds Devil, the painted kangaroo, the photograph
of the stuffed goat—all the evidence seems
to point to a *hoax*. A hoax is a prank or stunt
designed to capture the public's interest. Though
some people insist that the Jersey Devil is real,
most experts conclude the creature was created
and popularized by hoaxes.

Index

Written by Madeline King
Illustrations by Julian Baker, Familytree

Directed by Tom Evans
Edited by Jeff De La Rosa
Designed by Matt Carrington
Photo edited by Rosalia Bledsoe
Proofread by Nathalie Strassheim
Indexed by David Pofelski
Manufacturing led by Anne Fritzinger

World Book, Inc.
180 North LaSalle Street, Suite 900
Chicago, Illinois 60601
USA

For information about other World Book print and digital publications, please go to

www.worldbook.com or call 1-800-WORLDBK (967-5325).

For information about sales to schools and libraries,
call 1-800-975-3250 (United States) or 1-800-837-5365 (Canada).

Library of Congress Cataloging-in-Publication Data for this volume has been applied for.

Abnormal Field Guides to Cryptic Creatures
ISBN: 978-0-7166-4149-0 (set, hc.)

The Jersey Devil
ISBN: 978-0-7166-4154-4 (hc.)

Also available as:
ISBN: 978-0-7166-4162-9 (e-book)

Printed in the United States of America
by CG Book Printers, North Mankato, Minnesota
1st printing March 2020

© Dave Black: 33; © Getty Images: 7 (Neil Beckerman); © Dreamstime: 26 (Julie Feinstein);
Public Domain: 18; © The Kangaroo Sanctuary: 31; © Shutterstock: 5, 17, 19, 23-29, 34-37,
43, 45.

WORLD
BOOK
www.worldbook.com